All Scripture references taken from the KJV version of the Holy Bible, unless otherwise indicated.

Prayers Against Demonic Cobwebs

by Dr. Marlene Miles, 2023

Freshwater Press

ISBN: 978-1-960150-72-1

Copyright 2023 by Dr. Marlene Miles

All rights reserved. No part of this book may be reproduced, distributed or transmitted by any means or in any means including photocopying, recording or other electronic or mechanical methods without prior written permission of the publisher except in the case of brief publications or critical reviews.

Contents

Praise Unto Our God 5

Confess 9

Dreams & Warfare 11

Witchcraft Spiders 15

Triplet Demons 19

The Head 22

Attacks 25

Praise Strategy 33

Prayers Against the Triplet 34

Psalm 35 40

Cobwebs, Die 45

Fire, Fire, Fire! 50

Neutralize Cobweb Power 54

Barrenness, Fibroids, Impotence 57

Declare Blindness 62

My Luxury 67

Monitoring Webs 70

Foundations 73

Markets 76

Defang the Fangs! 79

I'm Not Your Food	83
Revealer of Secrets	92
Dear Reader	95
Other books by this author	96

Prayers Against Demonic Cobwebs

Praise Unto Our God

Lord, I declare, in the Name of Jesus that I am a born-again Protestant Christian, who is filled with the Holy Spirit of God.

I Praise You, Lord.

Psalm 145, *A psalm of praise of David.*

I will exalt you, my God the King; I will praise your name for ever and ever.

Every day I will praise you and extol your name for ever and ever.

Great is the LORD and most worthy of praise; his greatness no one can fathom.

One generation will commend your works to another; they will tell of your mighty acts.

They will speak of the glorious splendor of your majesty, and I will meditate on your wonderful works.

They will tell of the power of your awesome works, and I will proclaim your great deeds.

They will celebrate your abundant goodness and joyfully sing of your righteousness.

The Lord is gracious and compassionate, slow to anger and rich in love.

The Lord is good to all; he has compassion on all he has made.

All you have made will praise you, O Lord; your saints will extol you.

They will tell of the glory of your kingdom and speak of your might.

So that all men may know of your mighty acts and the glorious splendor of your kingdom.

Your kingdom is an everlasting kingdom, and your dominion endures through all generations. The Lord is faithful to all his promises and loving toward all he has made.

The Lord upholds all those who fall and lifts up all who are bowed down.

The eyes of all look to you, and you give them their food at the proper time.

You open your hand and satisfy the desires of every living thing.

The Lord is righteous in all his ways and loving toward all he has made.

The Lord is near to all who call on him, to all who call on him in truth.

He fulfills the desires of those who fear him; he hears their cry and saves them.

The Lord watches over all who love him, but all the wicked he will destroy.

My mouth will speak in praise of the Lord. Let every creature praise his holy name for ever and ever.

Amen.

Confess

Lord, I repent for every sin that I have ever committed against You, both sins of omission and commission. I repent of everything I've ever said or done that has grieved You, or grieved the Holy Spirit, in the Name of Jesus. I renounce and denounce that behavior; and I turn from my wicked ways. Lord, please forgive me, in the Name of Jesus.

I repent for my parents and also my ancestors all the way back before Adam and Even, in the Name of Jesus. Lord have Mercy on us.

Break every evil covenant that allows any curse to stand against me, in Jesus' Name.

Lord, break every bondage and yoke.

Lord, allow me to be covered by the Blood of the Covenant for this warfare, in Jesus' Name.

Dreams & Warfare

Hand of God, smack all the tools and devices that witches and wizards use against me out of the hands of every one of my enemies, and render them and their tools useless, in the Name of Jesus.

Blessing blockers, blessing stoppers, blessing thieves and hijackers--, not today, I am not the one, by the Power of the Holy Ghost in the Name of Jesus.

Devil, you will not make my house into a house of horrors; I will not walk into spider webs, cobwebs and such in my own house, in the Name of Jesus.

I refuse to be attacked by demonic cobwebs in my house or business, in the

Name of Jesus. Angels of God, stand guard to protect me and all the occupants of this house, in Jesus' Name.

My house is a house of goodness and it is dedicated to Jehovah God, it is the dwelling place of godliness. The visitation of angels is in my house, in the Name of Jesus.

Arachnophobia, fall down. Any and all *fear* I bind you and paralyze you now, in the Name of Jesus. You will not paralyze me; my Father has given me the spirit of love, power and a sound mind, in the Name of Jesus.

Through Christ, I am more than a conqueror, in Jesus' Name. Amen.

Thunder of God, locate and destroy every witchcraft attack against my life, family, house, and business, in the Name of Jesus.

Anyone using cobwebs to gain access into my life, fall down and die, in the Name of Jesus.

Lord, please don't let me be so complacent, lackadaisical, or ignorant that I don't see what needs to be seen; don't let me explain away important things as coincidence, in the Name of Jesus.

Lord, thank You for dreams that You give me and for proper, Christian, Biblical interpretation.

Holy Spirit, show me and help me pray to thwart the evil plans of the enemy against me, in the Name of Jesus.

Lord, help me remember all my dreams, in the Name of Jesus.

Help me to know the difference between an evil dream and a good dream, in Jesus' Name.

Lord, give me how to pray to bring forth the prophetic dreams of promise that You give me, by Your Spirit, in the Name of Jesus.

Thank You, Lord for new mercies every day. Thank You for daily loading us with benefits, in the Name of Jesus.

Lord of my breakthrough, remove every *spider spirit*, spider power, spider entity, spider man, spider woman from eyeing or attacking my blessings, breakthroughs and promotions, in the Name of Jesus.

Lord, reveal to me the source of constant and repeated disappointments and failures in my life, in the Name of Jesus.

Lord God, show me the real source of this battle, and help me to achieve a speedy victory against it, in the Name of Jesus.

Lord, give me Wisdom, Understanding and Grace to break the cords of the web in any demonic cobweb attack, in Jesus' Name.

Witchcraft Spiders

Lord, keep witchcraft spiders off my money, in the Name of Jesus. Give my money immunity from witchcraft theft, demonic manipulation and spider liquefaction, in the Name of Jesus.

In the natural and in the spiritual realm, Lord, give me the wherewithal, ability and knowledge to keep my house, office and environment clear of dust, cobwebs and spiderwebs, in the Name of Jesus.

Lord, give me the physical and spiritual acuity to recognize when something is out of place, out of order, or shouldn't even be in my environment, even a cobweb, in the Name of Jesus.

Witchcraft cobwebs, a demonic weapon used by the forces of darkness, especially witches—let your powers, enchantments and intentions against me fail and become harmless against me, in the Name of Jesus.

Every power using cobweb to try to initiate me into evil, lose your power against me, in the Name of Jesus. I reject your initiation and I break any evil covenant made knowingly, or unknowingly, by the power in the Blood of Jesus, in the Name of Jesus.

Anything put in me because of an evil initiation, I don't want it –, come up and out of me, now, in the Name of Jesus.

Lord, by Your Spirit, I reject evil summons, I reject every witchcraft covenant; I refuse to become any kind of witch or warlock, even a *blind witch*, in the Name of Jesus. **I refuse it.**

Lord, if I have become a *blind witch*, deliver me now, in the Name of Jesus. I repent for, renounce and denounce any witchcraft agreements, in Jesus' Name. Blood of Jesus transfuse me now, take out any trace of witchcraft blood in me, in Jesus' Name. Amen.

My soul, according to the Word of God I am to possess you in sanctification and honor; no cobweb can steal or imprison any part of my soul, by the power in the Blood of Jesus, in the Name of Jesus.

Every satanic agent, human or other, the Lord Jesus rebuke you and restrain you from attacking me in any way, in the Name of Jesus.

The Blood of Jesus is against you. I plead the Blood of Jesus, I proclaim that the Blood of Jesus is between you and me and you shall not pass by it, or through it, in the Name of Jesus.

Every satanic agent, principality, power, evil human agent, marine agent, night caterer, enchanter, diviner, and magician, be bound and paralyzed from operating against me, in the Name of Jesus. Amen.

I break your power to bring confusion, disappointment, failure, miscarriage, nightmares, isolation, loss, barrenness, and sorrow into my life, in the Name of Jesus.

By the power of God I release clarity, success, enjoyment, fruitfulness, Godly dreams, divine connections, divine relationships, and joy into my life; life and that more abundantly, by Jesus Christ. Amen.

Thank You, Lord, for You have given me power over all the works of Your hands. You have given me authority over snakes, scorpions and **spiders**, in the Name of Jesus. I trample them under my feet. I tread on them as the dust, in the Name of Jesus.

Triplet Demons

By the authority of Jesus Christ I address the triplet demons of the coven that are responsible for demonic cobweb attack, in the Name of Jesus.

Tobat, Hetbat, Melachat. I call down Holy Ghost Fire against your witchcraft altars, in the Name of Jesus.

You demons from the Marine Kingdom, the Lord preclude you from working against me in any way, by the Blood of Jesus.

You, *witchcraft spirits* hired to attack people with cobwebs, the Lord Jesus rebuke you. I bear in my body the marks of the Lord Jesus Christ and the Blood of Jesus prohibits you from attacking me, in the Name of Jesus.

Holy Ghost Fire, go on seek and find missions to find the launching places of those who send out demonic cobwebs for cobweb attack and singe them, scorch them, blast them, burn them, incinerate them with FIRE, FIRE, FIRE, Holy Ghost Fire--, to Oblivion, in the Name of Jesus.

Launching bases in any evil tree, cotton wool or any other tree–, receive the Thunder Fire of God, in Jesus' Name.

Take the voices of the evil three, LORD so they can't incant. Send forth confusion into their meeting so they can't agree, sow discord among them, in the Name of Jesus. Break up every voice of evil, in the Name of Jesus.

Lord, do not let the worship of the evil three be heard by their source of power, in the Name of Jesus.

Lord, put a wall of fire, a hedge of fire, a mountain of fire around me, protecting me against cobweb attack, in the Name of Jesus.

Any cobweb attack of the leg--, unravel, untangle, disentangle and go back to sender, in the Name of Jesus.

I proclaim breakthrough, success, and prosperity according to the Word of God and no one can stop it, in the Name of Jesus.

Let what they intended for me, Lord come upon them by a violent BACKFIRE, in the Name of Jesus.

Cobweb mask on the head or face, I nullify your power and enchantments over me, my head, my face, and my eyes and nose, in the Name of Jesus. You shall not capture my head, in Jesus' Name.

The Head

Lord, shield me from witchcraft cobweb attack of my face, in the Name of Jesus.

Lord, shield me from witchcraft cobweb attack of my head, in the Name of Jesus.

Lord, shield me from demonic cobweb attack of the hands, legs, or feet, in the Name of Jesus.

Lord, build a wall of fire around me to burn off all demonic cobwebs hurled against me, and as protection, light a hedge of fire, a mountain of fire against all cobweb attacks, in the Name of Jesus.

Every demonic, witchcraft cobweb attack – back to sender, 7-fold, in the Name of Jesus.

Lord, give me keen spiritual and physical vision to see the sometimes-subtle tactics of the devil, in the Name of Jesus.

I reject cobwebs over my eyes that is intended to hinder positive thought and good decisions, in the Name of Jesus. Lord, deliver me. Amen.

Blood of Jesus, locate my face, eyes, nose, every part of my head, and my destiny, by Fire, in the Name of Jesus.

Power of God unwrap my head from any web, cocoon, or evil covering, in the Name of Jesus; set me free.

Evil pronouncement made against my head, my life, I command you to lose your power, and loose me from your powers, in the Name of Jesus.

My head is set free from every bondage, in Jesus' Name.

Crown of good success stolen from me by cobweb attack--, Jesus, take it back.

Lord, let every dark or magical power hired against my destiny, fail, in Jesus' Name.

Helpers of my destiny, I am here; locate me with divine favor, in Jesus' Name.

Demonic cages hiding my true identity, break open now and let me go, in the Name of Jesus.

Lord, let me be celebrated where I have been rejected, in Jesus' Name.

Attacks

Overnight cobweb attacks planned and plotted, in the darkness, **fail** against me, in the Name of Jesus.

Street attacks, sudden cobweb attacks, fail; return to sender, in the Name of Jesus.

Cobweb attacks in the night, overnight, and/or in broad daylight, fail against me, in Jesus' Name.

Car attacks in the natural and regarding my vehicle of destiny, fail; return to sender, in the Name of Jesus.

Business attacks by demonic cobweb curses, fail; return to sender, in the Name of Jesus.

House attacks by evil cobweb projections, fail; return to sender, in the Name of Jesus.

Nature attacks while I'm out taking walks--, those that are not normal, fail against me. Return to sender, in the Name of Jesus.

Spiders, die. Spiders, die. Spider power die, witchcraft spider powers, die, in the Name of Jesus.

Triplet demon cobweb attacks –, you have been found out – I am no longer ignorant to your devices –, I command you to fail and leave my environment, and take your evil webs with you. Return to sender, in the Name of Jesus.

Return, return, return, return, return, return, return to your senders and attack them, instead of me, in the Name of Jesus.

You will not hold me down in one spot: backfire! *You* remain in one spot—not me, by Fire, in the Name of Jesus.

You will not make me stagnant; backfire – you be stagnant, in Jesus' Name.

You will not tie up my destiny; backfire – let your destiny receive what you intended for me, by the Power of Christ.

You will not trap me--, backfire! I command your webs to trap yourself, in the Name of Jesus.

You will not enslave my life or my spiritual life, I shall do the will of Him who sent me, to the Glory of God, in the Name of Jesus.

Man of War, Lord, release me from this net, trap and foul snare, in the Name of Jesus.

I will not miss my divine connections and destiny helpers because of cobweb attack spoiling my timeline, in the Name of

Jesus--, let your intent backfire and you miss out in your life, in the Name of Jesus.

Lord, give me knowledge of the devil's devices and Wisdom to act quickly, effectively, and successfully in a way that is pleasing to You, in the Name of Jesus.

Every trap to delay, to derail, divert, stop or interrupt my marriage, I cancel your power against me, by the power in the Blood of Jesus. Return to **sender**, in the Name of Jesus.

Bad luck, disfavor, disappointments, you have no longer have a home here --back to sender, in the Name of Jesus.

Hatred and reproach --, I am not your candidate, I walk in divine favor, the favor of my God who contends with those who contend with me, in the Name of Jesus.

Lord, raise up a formidable Adversary against my adversaries, in Jesus' Name.

Marital strife, division and divorce–, relationship troubles--, backfire --return to sender, in the Name of Jesus.

Business downturns, business loss or losses as a result of witchcraft or cobweb attack, will have no effect on me, instead, backfire, in the Name of Jesus.

Debt, projections of debt against my life – backfire, return to sender, in the Name of Jesus.

Career blockers, return to sender, Lord, give me divine favor in getting every job I apply for and even jobs that I don't apply for. Favorable and lucrative, Godly jobs and positions *find* me, in the Name of Jesus.

Ministry and ministry growth, attacked by cobwebs to cause members of a ministry to turn against the pastor, be canceled now, by the Blood of Jesus.

Cobweb attacks to cover a person's spiritual gifts, to cause people not to appreciate other people's gifts, I nullify your evil assignment against me now, in Jesus' Name.

Spiritual captivity – I'm not your candidate. Whom the Son sets free is free indeed... I am not your captive. I am not your prisoner. I am not your prey, not today, not any day, in the Name of Jesus.

Cobweb spider, I am not the sacrifice on your evil altar, the Blood of Jesus answers for me, in the Name of Jesus.

Cobwebs to try to render me useless, get to stepping, I have purpose and destiny, and by the Grace and the Power of God, I will fulfill it, in the Name of Jesus.

Lord, do not let me miss Your messages in my dreams and even in my waking life by Your signs and symbols, no matter how small they seem, *such as cobwebs*, in the Name of Jesus.

Do not let me think that anything that means something means nothing, in the Name of Jesus.

Triplet demonic spiritual cobweb attack I come against you in the Name of the Lord Jesus Christ who is a Man of War. I come against you with the Blood of Jesus, the Razor of the Lord, the Fiery Serpent, the Flaming Sword, the East Wind, hailstones of fire, tsunamis of Living Water and every other weapon the Lord allows me to use, until I achieve complete and total victory against you, in the Name of Jesus.

Powers attacking my life, die, in the Name of Jesus.

Holy Ghost Fire, KILL the spiders, KILL the spiders, Kill the spiders, in the Name of Jesus.

I dismantle your cobwebs and every power associated or assigned to the webs, in the Name of Jesus.

I scatter your mission and command it to never re-assemble against me again, in the Name of Jesus.

I break you off from your network. I block you from getting any reinforcements against me, and command you to fall down and die, and not be teleported back to your base, lose all connection with your base, and die, in the Name of Jesus. It's over.

Deliver me, O Lord, in the Name of Jesus. Reverse all captivity, reverse all damage and restore everything stolen and taken from me, in the Name of Jesus.

Cobweb attacks, I break your power to bring untimely death to me or anything in my life, from possessions, to relationships, in the Name of Jesus, by the power in the Blood of Jesus.

Praise Strategy

I will praise You Lord, for you are Worthy to be praised. I will meditate on Your Word, and offer prayers to you day after day, night after night until I receive my deliverance, in the Name of Jesus. Amen.

I give thanks to You, Lord.

I sing Praises unto the Lord. Give thanks for Your Mercy and Your lovingkindness toward us, Amen.

(Pray these prayers from midnight to 3:00 AM for four days consecutively is best. Fast for 7 days, if possible 6am to 6pm. If you cannot do that, fast your favorite food/beverage for 30 days.)

Prayers Against the Triplet

All glory-destroying witchcraft orchestrated by Tobat cobwebs in any area of my life and my family's life, be consumed by the *Fire* of the Blood of Jesus.

Every *spirit* tracking my movement for advancement in my life through Melachat cobwebs, be destroyed, in the Name of Jesus.

You, my vision of glory, under bewitchment and manipulation by Hetbat Cobwebs, be destroyed by the Fire of the Blood of Jesus.

Every stronghold in my life by the triplet demons known as Tobat, Melachat, and Hetbat be uprooted and demolished, in the Name of Jesus.

Every evil spirit orchestrated from the 35th plain of the Marine Kingdom and powered by the triplet demons Tobat, Melachat, & Hetbat, to destroy my breakthroughs, be consumed by the power in the Blood of Jesus.

My Glory, my Vision, my progress in life, under bewitchment and monitoring by the triplet witchcraft cobwebs--, be redeemed by the Blood of Jesus.

Every evil, witchcraft, covenant, and monitor teleported through the triplet cobweb networks, affecting my existence, and that of my family, be broken, and *loose* your hold, and lose your hold, in the Name of Jesus.

You, Tobat, Hetbat, Melachat demons using witchcraft cobwebs to monitor me and any members of my family in the physical, destroying or delaying breakthroughs and blessings, I command you to die!, in the Name of Jesus.

My ministerial call and my ministry under lockdown by Satanic triplet cobweb demons, be set free and be redeemed, by the power in the Blood of Jesus.

Any stronghold in my life orchestrated by the triplet cobweb demons known as Tobat, Melachat, Hetbat, *loose* your hold, lose your hold, by Fire by Force, in the Name of Jesus.

All demonic, spiritual monitors empowered by the Tobat, Melachat, Hetbat cobwebs, be consumed by the Fire of the Holy Ghost, in the Name of Jesus.

Every spiritual cobweb in the personality of Tobat, Melachat, and Hetbat that is covering my beauty, my glory and affecting my relationships--, I call upon the God of Elijah, who answers by Fire, to consume you to ashes, in the Name of Jesus.

If my business is under the bewitchment of spiritual cobweb demons, in the personalities of Tobat, Melachat and Hetbat. I command Fire from Heaven to consume every web and restore my business to its former glory, even growing more successful to the Glory of God, in the Name of Jesus.

My Glory and breakthroughs under siege by the Triplet Cobweb Demons, Tobat, Melachat, and Hetbat, be released by the judgment of God, in the Name of Jesus.

Let their demonic cobwebs be consumed by Fire of the Holy Ghost, in the Name of Jesus Christ.

Every cobweb assigned against my glory, my vision, my movement, my success, I command the triplet demons or anything empowering them to be paralyzed now, in Jesus Name.

Every Tobat cobweb targeted at my vision, die by Fire, in the mighty Name of Jesus Christ.

Every Melachat cobweb assigned to waste my efforts in life, I command you to roast by Fire, in the Name of Jesus.

Every group of witches using my name and my mother's name written on their evil blackboard, known as VUNC and by the evil writer known as LETUVUNC to attack me, let the Fire of God consume you all to ashes, in the Name of Jesus.

Any power making me repeat prayer points without getting answers, God rebuke you, in His anger and in His hot displeasure, in the Name of Jesus.

Every aspect of my life and family that Satan has frustrated through the triplet demon cobwebs, Lord Almighty fight for me and destroy all my enemies, in the Name of Jesus.

Every council of three witchcraft men resulting in cobwebs, I declare a consuming Fire of God, to set you ablaze and for you to incinerate to ashes, in the Name of Jesus.

Any evil caused by triplet demon cobwebs in my life and loved ones, I reverse it back to good and favor, for both me and my loved ones, in the Name of Jesus.

As from this moment and this day, I decree, no spiritual cobwebs will work against me, my business, my marriage, my relationships, my ministry, my education, my career or profession, my health, or any of the members of my household ever again, in the Name of Jesus. Amen.

Psalm 35

Plead my cause, O LORD, with them that strive with me: fight against them that fight against me.

Take hold of shield and buckler, and stand up for mine help.

Draw out also the spear, and stop the way against them that persecute me: say unto my soul, I am thy salvation.

Let them be confounded and put to shame that seek after my soul: let them be turned back and brought to confusion that devise my hurt.

Let them be as chaff before the wind: and let the angel of the LORD chase them.

Let their way be dark and slippery: and let the angel of the LORD persecute them.

For without cause have they hid for me their net in a pit, which without cause they have digged for my soul.

Let destruction come upon him at unawares; and let his net that he hath hid catch himself: into that very destruction let him fall.

And my soul shall be joyful in the LORD: it shall rejoice in his salvation.

All my bones shall say, LORD, who is like unto thee, which deliverest the poor from him that is too strong for him, yea, the poor and the needy from him that spoileth him?

False witnesses did rise up; they laid to my charge things that I knew not.

They rewarded me evil for good to the spoiling of my soul.

But as for me, when they were sick, my clothing was sackcloth: I humbled my soul with fasting; and my prayer returned into mine own bosom.

I behaved myself as though he had been my friend or brother: I bowed down heavily, as one that mourneth for his mother.

But in mine adversity they rejoiced, and gathered themselves together: yea, the abjects gathered themselves together against me, and I knew it not; they did tear me, and ceased not:

With hypocritical mockers in feasts, they gnashed upon me with their teeth.

Lord, how long wilt thou look on? rescue my soul from their destructions, my darling from the lions.

I will give thee thanks in the great congregation: I will praise thee among much people.

Let not them that are mine enemies wrongfully rejoice over me: neither let them wink with the eye that hate me without a cause.

For they speak not peace: but they devise deceitful matters against them that are quiet in the land.

Yea, they opened their mouth wide against me, and said, Aha, aha, our eye hath seen it.

This thou hast seen, O LORD: keep not silence: O Lord, be not far from me.

Stir up thyself, and awake to my judgment, even unto my cause, my God and my Lord.

Judge me, O LORD my God, according to thy righteousness; and let them not rejoice over me.

Let them not say in their hearts, Ah, so would we have it: let them not say, We have swallowed him up.

Let them be ashamed and brought to confusion together that rejoice at mine hurt: let them be clothed with shame and dishonour that magnify themselves against me.

Let them shout for joy, and be glad, that favour my righteous cause: yea, let them say continually, Let the LORD be magnified, which hath pleasure in the prosperity of his servant.

And my tongue shall speak of thy righteousness and of thy praise all the day long.

(Bless a bottle of water with this Psalm and sprinkle it throughout your house.)

Cobwebs, Die

Power using cobwebs to attack my destiny, die, in the Name of Jesus.

I chase out any evil spirit lurking around my house, in the Name of Jesus.

Every witchcraft agent using cobwebs to attack my prayer life, die, in the Name of Jesus.

Cobweb power stopping good news in my life, scatter by fire, in the Name of Jesus.

Oh God, arise and let my prayer kill all my enemies, in the Name of Jesus, Amen.

Their web shall not become garments, neither shall they cover themselves with their works. Their works are works of iniquity, and the act of violence is in their hands. (Isaiah 59:6)

Every cobweb power blocking me physically and spiritually – blocking my progress in any way, catch Fire, in the Name of Jesus. Amen.

He made a pit, and digged it, and is fallen into the ditch which he made. His mischief shall return upon his own head, and his violent dealing shall come down upon his own pate. (Psalm 7:14-15)

I challenge every power spinning cobwebs to trap my destiny, in the Name of Jesus.

Any wicked human agents using spider webs to trouble my destiny, die by Fire, in the Name of Jesus.

You, spider of darkness assigned to bring problems to me, I bind you and paralyze you today, in the Name of Jesus.

Every household strongman using cobwebs to oppose me, block me, or set a trap for me, be roasted by Fire, in the Name of Jesus.

I release myself from every curse of cobweb working against me, in the Name of Jesus.

Every wicked person that wants to imprison my destiny with cobwebs be roasted by Fire, in the Name of Jesus.

Cobweb powers in my house, workplace, and community I set you ablaze with Holy Ghost Fire, in the Name of Jesus.

My star, my glory, my destiny stolen by witchcraft spiders, you cannot escape, return my star, my glory, and my destiny to me, and then die, in the Name of Jesus.

Every satanic trap set for me through spiderwebs, spider dreams, spider web dreams, catch fire, in the Name of Jesus.

Any witchcraft house harbouring spider webs to delay and cage my life, I set you ablaze, in the Name of Jesus.

Anyone sponsoring or fueling any cobweb attack against me, Fire of God disgrace them, in the Name of Jesus.

I cancel and overcome the power of darkness over my life, in the Name of Jesus.

Any part of my body in contact with evil spiders, webs, receive deliverance, in the Name of Jesus.

Every evil ever done to my life through cobweb attack, be reversed by Fire, in the Name of Jesus.

I break myself loose from every bondage of cobweb covenant, in the Name of Jesus.

My trust is in You, Lord, not in chariots, horses or fragile things such as spider's webs, but in You. Lord, deliver me, in the matchless Name of Jesus Christ.

Every evil cobweb: Lose your power. Lose your power. Lose your power, Lose your power against me, in the Name of Jesus.

Evil enchantments on any witchcraft net, web, spiderweb, cobweb, BACKFIRE, in the Name of Jesus. I send you on the Wind of God back to your sender. Capture your sender, not me, in Jesus' Name.

Fire, Fire, Fire!

God of Elijah, let Fire fall from Heaven and burn to ashes any and every demonic cobweb in my life, family, household or business causing delays in any area of our lives, in Jesus' Name.

I burn your silk; I light it up with Holy Ghost Fire.

I burn your highways, your routes, I light them up with the Fire of the Holy Ghost.

Lord, send recovery angels to go both to the seen and the unseen worlds and recover everything that was stolen from me. Have them search the land of the living and the dead and bring back everything taken from me or my family as a result of coming into contact with demonic cobwebs, from birth to now--, all of our lives, even when we were ignorant of their devices, in Jesus' Name.

Lord, redeem the time; restore the years, in the Name of Jesus.

Father, send Your Warrior Angels to go to both the seen and the unseen worlds, to completely remove any demonic cobweb traps of delay, disappointment, loss, barrenness, poverty, covering or affliction of any kind, used to prevent destiny helpers from locating me, in Jesus' Name.

Lord, let every demonic cobweb put into my life by any demonic boss, landlord, wicked family member, friends, fake friends, ex's, or current relationships --, enemies unknown to me, and/or occultic groups to steal my prosperity, health, destiny, and other valuables at any time, ever in my life, backfire, in Jesus' Name.

Lord, let me recover all, as David recovered all at Ziklag, in the Name of Jesus.

Lord, let the Fire of the Holy Ghost burn to ashes every satanic cobweb that the enemy is using to cover my progress, my good works and even my hard work so I am not recognized or successful and honored with promotion, in Jesus' Name.

Promotion comes from You, Lord; let me walk in Your Divine Favor always, in the Name of Jesus.

By the power in the Name of Jesus, I decree and declare total destruction of every demonic cobweb of poverty, in Jesus' Name.

In the Name of Jesus, I command every demonic cobweb upon me and my family that is attracting evil, shame, or pain, to catch Fire, in Jesus' Name.

Lord, I pray that You will save me and my family from every evil affliction that came as a result of cobweb attacks, in the Name of Jesus.

Let the power of the Holy Ghost give me speed this year in everything. I break free from any satanic cobweb especially one of stagnation, and I move forward in my divine assignment, in Jesus' Name.

Neutralize Cobweb Power

I nullify and neutralize the magnetic power of every demonic cobweb, in the Name of Jesus, whether I come into contact with it or not, I render it neutral, useless, and powerless, and harmless against me, in the Name of Jesus.

Lord, let the intent of every cobweb that has been sent against me in my household, my business, my life, and the life of my family, backfire! Return to sender, in the Name of Jesus, by the power in the Name of Jesus.

I decree and declare total destruction of all evil powers using demonic cobwebs that have vowed to keep me in the same job, same house, same place, trudging along the same path and career for the rest of my life without progress, in Jesus' Name. You're a liar; I shall progress and reach the destiny that God has planned for me from the Beginning.

By the power in the Name of Jesus, let every demonic cobweb break into irreparable pieces, in the Name of Jesus.

Father, send Your Warrior Angels with swords drawn locate and completely destroy all demonic cobwebs on any doors, rooms, roads, windows, public places, and any other spaces where these wiry traps have been set to trap me or my family, in the Name of Jesus.

By the power in the Name of Jesus, I decree and declare destruction of every demonic cobweb of poverty, sickness, infirmity, backwardness, setbacks, stagnation, disappointment, confusion, hatred, rejection, reproach, non-achievement, barrenness, failure, and any covering over my life, myself, or my family, in the Name of Jesus.

Let every demonic power that is using spiritual cobwebs to steal from me, store, and eventually divert my God-given blessings to a demonic storehouse, fall down and die, in the Name of Jesus.

By the power in the Name of Jesus, I decree and declare that whosoever would try to reactivate these demonic cobwebs and spider stings that have hindered my ancestors and my parents from succeeding in life, let them be destroyed by Fire, in Jesus' Name. Return to sender!

Barrenness, Fibroids, Impotence

I burn your silk; I light it up with Holy Ghost Fire.

I burn your highways, your routes, I light them up with the Fire of the Holy Ghost.

Silk Trade Routes in the Spirit–, spiritual silk routes, I annihilate, I bombard you, I use the weapons from the armory of God, the treasury of His weapons and I ignite, incinerate, cut, shave, raze, destroy, disconnect, confuse, melt and zap the power of your silk routes that involve me in any way, and render them null, void, useless and ineffective, in Jesus' Mighty Name.

Forget my name, lose my location, receive Holy Ghost Smoke, Holy Ghost Fire and mass confusion now, in the Name of Jesus.

Lord, let the Blood of Jesus wash me clean of every demonic sickness, affliction, and infirmity caused by coming into contact with any demonic cobweb, in the Name of Jesus.

Mercy, Lord – I cry for Mercy –

I come against barrenness. Fallopian tube blockage as a result of cobweb attack, be disentangled now and my tubes become patent to work as God intended, in the Name of Jesus.

Agent of darkness who caused barrenness of any kind, in my life, receive Judgment for messing with a child of God, in the Name of Jesus.

Mercy Lord, I cry Mercy –

Fibroids as a result of cobweb attack, be melted, dissolved and expelled now, or miraculously, spiritually, surgically excised by the hand of the Great Physician, in the Name of Jesus.

Every Satanic arrow projected into my womb, return back to sender, back to sender, back to sender, sevenfold, in the mighty Name of Jesus.

Cobwebs of miscarriage in pregnant women, or delay and even getting pregnant, lose your power against my womb immediately, in Jesus' Name.

Lord, reverse all symptoms and damage of fibroids in the bodies of Your children, in the Name of Jesus.

Agent of darkness who caused the fibroid(s) receive the judgment of God now for harming a child of God, in the Name of Jesus. Amen.

Impotence and/or low sperm count, as a result of cobweb attack, let every constriction and entanglement become untangled now, in the Name of Jesus.

Agent of darkness responsible for this malady – go to the Abyss. You've been found out; I declare **failed assignment**, go to the Abyss where there is no water and there is no return, in the Name of Jesus.

Any satanic web purposing to lock my womb be neutralized now, in the Name of Jesus.

RIGHTEOUS SEED OF THE LORD, COME FORTH, COME FORTH, IN THE NAME OF JESUS.

Every cobweb attack to cover me with shame or to cover me from divine connections, destiny helpers, Godly relationships and/or Kingdom marriage, I break you with the Fire Machete of God and call for the East Wind of God to blow you into Oblivion never to be regathered, reassembled, or reconstituted, in the Name of Jesus.

I break your three-fold cord, I break your cord within a cord, within a cord, by the Holy Fire of God, in Jesus' Name.

Declare Blindness

I speak blindness to your *spider*, forever, in the Name of Jesus. Every eye blind, every eye blind, forevermore, in the Name of Jesus.

Any demonic cobweb attacking my legs or feet, designed to **drag** me places where I should not go--, places I do not want to go, I reverse your effects and I command <u>**you**</u> to be dragged by the Holy Ghost. And by the Warrior Angels of God, in the Name of Jesus.

I curse any demonic web and it's sender that has ever wrapped around my legs or feet and caused me or my family member to fall, in the natural or in the spirit. I send you back to sender, back to sender, in the Name of Jesus. Amen.

Lord, reverse any damage in my body or life from any satanic, physical fall, in the Name of Jesus.

Lord, in the Name of Jesus, let any net that is spread for my feet, return on the sender, that they will be captured by their own enterprise, in the Name of Jesus.

In the Name of Jesus, Lord whosoever has hidden a cobweb in my path, waiting to ensnare my feet, they will fall into their own net, and I will not be caught in it, or fall, in the Name of Jesus.

Lord, let every pit digger that has hidden a net and a pit for me, let them fall into their own pit by Fire and by Force, in the Name of Jesus.

Lord, let every pit digger be buried by Fire, in the Name of Jesus.

Lord, let every *spider spirit* hunting my life be discomfited by Your lightning, and electrocuted by the power of the Holy Ghost, in the Name of Jesus Christ, Amen.

Blessings of Heaven fall on me now. Embellish me with glory and beauty, all the days of my life, in the majestic Name of Jesus Christ.

Finger of Fire, rewrite my story for glory. Lord, help me to fulfill destiny, in Jesus' Name.

Angels of God keep my feet from stumbling into the trap of any cobweb, in the Name of Jesus.

Glory of God, shine on my face. Let your light shine upon me, in Jesus' Name.

Scatter any cobweb purposed to steal my glory, in the Name of Jesus Christ. Lord, be a lamp unto my feet and a light unto my path so that I *see* the traps of the enemy before even approaching them, in the Name of Jesus.

Father, thank You that You load me with daily benefits, in the Name of Jesus.

Any spider scanning my blessings and my **daily** God-given benefits, to plunder them first, go blind by Fire, in the Name of Jesus.

I place a scourging curse on any spider person, especially any household spider person bent on spiritual violence against me, in the Name of Jesus Christ.

Jehovah Gibbor, preserve my prosperity by Fire, in the Name of Jesus.

Lord, I proclaim an end to any spider-person trying to liquify my blessings, and an end to his satanic eye monitoring my life. I pierce you with the Sword of God by the unapproachable, blinding Light of God, in the Name of Jesus.

I crush all eyeballs that are monitoring me from the demonic realm, in the Name of Jesus.

Any cobweb being used as CCTV cameras in my life, I blacken your screens, blind your eyes, and unplug you from your every power source, by a Holy Ghost power surge, in the Name of Jesus.

Let your devices and gadgets fail now, in Jesus' Name.

Every spider eye, spiritual or natural, eyeing my inheritance, spiritual or natural, **BURST!** in the Name of Jesus.

Lord with Holy Ghost slap, punish the eyes of any *spider spirit* eyeing my benefits and blessings that You have sent and intend for me, ***daily***, in the Name of Jesus.

My Luxury

Any *spider spirit*, spider man, spider woman, any spider *entity* living in luxury at my expense, vomit up all you've stolen from me, pay me back 7-fold what you've taken from me, then somersault and die, in the Name of Jesus.

Any cage holding my blessings, break, Break! **BREAK!**, in the Name of Jesus.

Hand of Fire, Hand of God, release my destiny now, in the Name of Jesus.

Lord, keep witchcraft spiders off my money, in the Name of Jesus. Give my money immunity from witchcraft theft, demonic manipulation and spider liquefaction, in the Name of Jesus.

Family cobweb attack, I break your powers over my family now, in the Name of Jesus.

By the power in the Blood of Jesus, I break the evil covenant that allows the presence of evil cobwebs in our family; I bind and paralyze the demon that is in place to enforce any curse, and we walk free, by the Blood of Jesus, in the Name of Jesus.

We break free of any cobweb that is holding us captive for any reason in any witchcraft coven, by the Blood of Jesus.

Neighborhood cobweb attack, I break your powers over my neighborhood and street now, in the Name of Jesus by the Power in the Blood of Jesus.

Cobwebs holding my state or country I come against you in the Name of the Lord God, whom you defy. You will be dismantled and defeated, in the Name of Jesus.

Every power attempting to translate or exchange my glory, breakthroughs, blessings and successes, fail miserably, and lose your power, in the Name of Jesus.

Every spider--, fishing spider or trapdoor spider – DIE! DIE! DIE! in the Name of Jesus.

Monitoring Webs

Every wicked man monitoring my life to slay me, your time has come, breathe your last, and die, in the mighty Name of Jesus.

Lord, reveal to me how the enemy knows what I am doing when I haven't told anyone, in the Name of Jesus.

Any spider man weaving a web against me, die, in the Name of Jesus!

Any monitoring cobweb observing and reporting on my life to *spider spirits*, I smite you with the Fiery Sword of God, in the Name of Jesus.

Every spiritual monitor operating through household witchcraft agents, drawing powers from the 35th Plane of the Marine Kingdom, affecting my life, I ask the Rock of Ages smash them into pieces, in the Name of Jesus.

Spiritual entities behind demonic webs, you cannot hide anymore--, die now, in the Name of Jesus.

Every agent of darkness who's using spiritual cobwebs to monitor my going in, and coming out in order to destroy my upcoming breakthroughs, let the wrath of God consume them.

Let their demonic cobwebs be consumed by Fire of the Holy Ghost, in the Name of Jesus Christ.

Blood of Christ, enforce my dominion, by Fire.

Lord, activate the speaking Blood of Jesus in my life, in the Name of Jesus.

My God, my refuge, cleanse my house of spider evil, spider people, spider curses, spider burglars, spider webs, cobwebs, and spider traps.

By the sprinkling of the Blood of Jesus--, I overcome every foe by the Blood of the Covenant, in the Name of Jesus. Amen.

Spear of the Lord, pierce any evil eye coveting my blessings, in the Name of Jesus.

Foundations

Great Foundation, establish my feet, in Your Name.

Let the evil foundations of my father's house be confounded now, by the Name of Jesus. Evil foundations of my father's house, my mother's house, dissolve now by Fire, in the Name of Jesus.

By my covenant right, in the Name of Jesus, I establish righteous foundations in my family, in the Name of Jesus, Amen.

Cornerstone of Zion, let my foundations be in perfect harmony with You; arrange my life with great glory now, in Jesus' Name.

In the Name of Jesus, I crush every evil foundation being employed by witches to my harm. All evil ministers at any evil altar, any evil foundation of my family, somersault and die, in the Name of Jesus.

Blood of Christ burn before me, and behind me, turn the land of my enemies into a desolate wilderness, in Jesus' Name.

Stronghold of life, give me double for my trouble, in the Name of Jesus, by the Blood of the Covenant.

Lord, break any prison hold in my life; rescue me from my enemy/enemies, in the Name of Jesus.

Acidic rain from Heaven, rain in the camp of *spider spirits* now, in Jesus' Name.

Lord, shake up every meeting place of triplet demons, by Fire and by Thunder and run them out of their meeting places, in the Name of Jesus.

Bombard them with hailstones of Holy Ghost Fire, in the Name of Jesus.

Liquid Fire from Heaven, fall on them now, in the mighty Name of Jesus.

Markets

Lord, invade the witchcraft markets on my behalf now, in the Name of Jesus.

Lord, by Your angels, cause their markets to fail by Fire, in the Name of Jesus.

Lord, by the power of Christ and the Blood of Jesus, ransom any captured part of me from every evil, witchcraft market, in the Name of Jesus.

My destiny, I call you back from the evil marketplace; you will not be sold, you will not be bought, in Jesus' Name. I call you back to me by the Fire power of the Blood of Jesus.

Any item of my destiny displayed on the witchcraft market, be removed, be recovered by the hand of God, in Jesus' powerful Name.

Every contract assigned on my head in the witchcraft market--, fail. I set those papers on fire by the power and the Fire of the Holy Ghost, in Jesus' Name. Amen.

God of Peace, crush the head of Satan and every enemy of my life under my feet. Bring them to an utter end, in Jesus Name.

Any adversary leering at any open door of my life, let every dimensional access point be shut, closed and sealed against demonic interlopers, and let those enemies be apprehended by the Warrior Angels of God, and taken to where the True Lord Jesus has for them, in the Name of Jesus.

Any item of my destiny that is currently for sale in any witchcraft market, I command it to jump out of that market, in the Name of Jesus.

By the fear of my covering, Jesus Christ, Lord, let the witchcraft market where my goods have been displayed be trampled by the war horses of God, and I recover all my goods now, with angelic help, by Force, in Jesus' Name.

Angels of God retrieve my belongings, the things of my destiny, wash them with Living Water and return them to me, in the Name of Jesus.

Lord, let every evil assignment against my life and my peace be expired now, by Thunder in Jesus' Name.

Defang the Fangs!

Wrath of God, fall on my adversaries now, by Fire, in the Name of Jesus.

Any spider fangs targeted at me: I command you to break! Break! Break! in the Name of Jesus; I defang you by the power of the Thunder Hammer of God.

Thunder Hammer of God, crush the jaws of any *spider spirit* trying to liquify my blessings, and have their venom turn on them and poison them, in the Name of Jesus.

Every witchcraft spider and web, scatter by Fire, scatter by Fire, scatter by Fire.

You, *spider spirit* and every entity behind the demonic cobweb, somersault and die, in the Name of Jesus.

My Father, my Fighter, my Creator, My Lord. Show me great Mercy now; turn my afflictions and sorrows to gladness, let everything the devil meant for my harm be turned to my good, in the Name of Jesus.

Evil spiders, I defang your fangs by the Spirit of God.

I render harmless your venom except to backfire on you; liquefy **yourself**, in the Name of Jesus.

Every trap by means of a spider web assigned to cage my destiny, catch your owner, instead of me, by Fire, in the Name of Jesus.

Workers of mischief and iniquity, die, and let your works return back to you. Let them be on your own head, in the Name of Jesus Christ.

Destiny Helper(s) come into my life by Fire, in the Name of Jesus.

Any witch--, household or otherwise, after my glory, your time has come--, expire now, in the Name of Jesus.

Strongman of war, overturn any evil verdict against my life by Fire. Lord, scatter any witchcraft market where a price tag has been placed on my head, in the Name of Jesus.

Angels of God, war against the adversary/adversaries of my progress, and establish **my** victory at the gates of my enemies, in the Name of Jesus Christ.

My Father, my Fighter, give me the gates of my enemies, empower my hands to take them for a spoil, in Jesus' Name.

Lord, give me the necks of my enemies and empower me to take them for spoil, in the Name of Jesus.

Any *spider spirit* opposing God's prophetic agenda for my life, expire now, check out of my life right now, in the mighty Name of Jesus Christ.

I'm Not Your Food

Right Hand of God, arise for me now and smite any contrary power, in Jesus' Name.

Power of *spider spirits* in my workplace, in my house, in my life, in my body, perish, in the Name of Jesus Christ.

Lord, bring my enemies to a screeching halt, and overthrow their works and all their progress against me, now, in the Name of Jesus.

Spider spirit, spider man, spider woman, I am not your candidate; **I am not your food,** I am not your meat, in Jesus' Name.

I neutralize the power of any cobweb in my path, in my way, in the Name of Jesus.

Spider spirit, spider man, spider woman, I am not your sacrifice, I break free by Jesus Christ.

You--, eat your own flesh, drink your own blood and die, in the Name of Jesus.

Every *spider spirit* seeking after my life, be electrocuted by the Thunder Lightning of the Holy Ghost, in the Name of Jesus.

I anoint every door of my house and the four corners of my room, Lord. And, I decree and declare that the charges of any cobweb set as a trap for me are neutralized against me, in the Name of Jesus.

I break out of every cobweb cage, in the Name of Jesus.

Lord Jesus my Covering--, coverer of my head. Show up for me now, and with your strong hand of power, shield me from the webs of the web-spinning evil spider men, triplet demons, and evil human agents who don't mind inflicting harm on God's people, in the Name of Jesus.

Terror of death fall in the camp of my enemies now, have them run away in utter astonishment, in the Name of Jesus.

My Father, God, terrorize any *spider spirit* after my destiny, in the Name of Jesus. Voice of the Lord's Thunder, thunder in any witchcraft coven where my name is being mentioned. Terrorize them by the wrath of God, in the Name of Jesus.

Mighty One of Israel, shake your hands over my life, Lord, smite every trace of cobweb and get it out of my life, forever, in Jesus' Name.

Manipulation in my life, STOP now, in the Name of Jesus Christ.

By the shaking of hands I reign over all my enemies, by Jesus Christ.

By the winds of God, Lord, frustrate evil cobwebs targeted against me, in Jesus' Name.

By the eternal Sword of God I cut off any spider hands being used to fashion any evil against me, in Jesus' Name.

Every shooting spider that is shooting arrows, lose your direction, lose your target, and if it's me or mine that you're shooting at, lose my location and forget my name, in the Name of Jesus.

Flaming Sword of God visit any *spider spirit*, spider power, spider entity, spider man, spider woman working against my life now, in the Name of Jesus. Anger of God, visit my enemies with a vengeance.

Lord, do not restrain Yourself; pour out Your wrath on them, in the Name of Jesus.

Traffic on my head in the night seasons, you must be from God and Holy Ghost inspired, in Jesus' Name. All other traffic, go back to the pit from whence you came, in the Name of Jesus.

Voice of the Blood of Jesus by force, by dominion, and by Fire, neutralize the charges of any cobweb set as a trap against me, in the Name of Jesus Christ.

Holy Spiders of Heaven, release webs from my Father, now, and ensnare the wicked man who's trying to ensnare me. Ensnare the wicked man who has set traps and snares in my path, in the Name of Jesus.

Bring their works to nothing, by Fire, in the Name of Jesus.

Any mask on the face of my enemies, fall off, burn off, in the Name of Jesus. Fall off, fall off by Fire, Fall off by Fire, fall off.

Every cobweb being used as a mask, catch Fire, in the Name of Jesus.

Sword of God attack the enemies of my destiny and progress in my life, in the Name of Jesus.

Any spider leg that is trying to come in my direction catch fire now. By Holy Ghost Fire, in the Name of Jesus, I rid all you evil spiders coming against me, of all of your legs. Lose control, roll over, and die, in the Name of Jesus.

Any pit digger in my family—household witchcraft, stand down, or fall in your own pit, in Jesus' Name..

Hand of Fire, God's Consuming Fire, secure my inheritance against corruption, Hide me from every evil eye in or out of my family, in the Name of Jesus.

Warring Angels of God. bring this battle to an end, please, Lord, bring my spoils now, in the Name of Jesus.

Godly Spiders of Heaven, defeat the tokens of my enemies now; render them null, void, and powerless, in Jesus' Name.

Every Satanic family gathering with the purpose to deliver me to poverty, scatter now by Thunder, scatter by Fire, in the Name of Jesus.

Spiders of Heaven, visit my enemies now. Turn their works on their own heads. Liquify their instruments of divination against me, in the Name of Jesus.

Vengeance of God, show up in the camp of my enemies now; visit their previous iniquity coupled with their intentions against me; let them drink the cup of their works of evil, in the Name of Jesus.

Lord of All, rule over all my fears.

Righteous Judge, speak in my favor, now, with Jesus as my Advocate and the Blood of the Covenant as my defense, rule in my favor against my enemies.

Lord, release Your fiery verdict against the *spider spirits* that are up against my life.

My life, receive Fire, become Fire, by Fire, in the Name of Jesus.

Righteous Judge, cause every viper after my life to drink its own venom, its own poison--, and die, in the Name of Jesus.

Lord, cause the internal organs of every evil viper, every evil serpent to be trapped by Fire, in the Name of Jesus.

My Father, My Shield, hide me from the evil net of evil fishermen and fisher spiders. Let their net remain forever empty as it concerns me, in the Name of Jesus.

Lord, hide me in the cleft of Your Rock, in the Name of Jesus.

Divine Light of God, open my eyes to see what the human eye cannot see. Let no good thing be hidden from my eyes, in the Name of Jesus.

By the power of the Holy Ghost, I defile the masked masquerades. Unmask them, Lord, in the Name of Jesus.

Touch them with their own abominations; return to sender, in the Name of Jesus.

Sword of the Lord, cut off the hands of any spider, spider man, *spider spirit*, man, woman, any satanic agent in my environment, in the Name of Jesus.

I live free of cobweb manipulation, in the Name of Jesus.

Whom the Son sets free is free, indeed. Amen.

Revealer of Secrets

Lord, You are the revealer of secrets. Light the realm of the Spirit before me, give me Wisdom to understand the workings of the spirit realm, in the Name of Jesus.

By the power of the Holy Ghost, my sleep is open for heavenly transactions only. I am open to Godly visitations and dreams. I have many heavenly, Godly encounters in my sleep, in the Name of Jesus.

Lion of Judah, ROAR! in the camp of witchcraft covens where anything concerning me is being cooked.

Discomfort them utterly with Your Thunder and Your lightnings, in Jesus' Name.

Any accident intended for me by means of the dragnet, I escape, I escape. I escape every incident, accident, mishap, illness, sickness, disorder, poverty, loss, disappointment, affliction, or temptation. This year--, I escape, I escape, I escape, in the Name of Jesus, Amen.

Lord, thank You for hearing and answering these prayers, in the Name of Jesus.

Lord, I proclaim and claim recovery of everything stolen from me by *spider spirits* through their demonic devices and webs in the Name of Jesus for **ALL** of my life up unto this point.

Lord, don't let me suffer for things that I didn't even know anything about, in the Name of Jesus.

I bind up and paralyze every revengeful, retaliatory demon, entity, power or principality that would come against me because of these prayers, and I paralyze them from any attack, in the Name of Jesus.

I seal these declarations across every age, dimension and timeline, past present and future, to infinity, in the Name of Jesus.

I seal every possible access opening against my life, future, destiny, ministry, marriage, family and purpose by the Blood of Jesus and the Seal of the Holy Spirit of Promise.

AMEN.

Dear Reader:

Thank you for purchasing and reading this book. Your support of this ministry means so much to me. May the Spirit of God continue to minister to you through the words of this book as well as ongoing in your life.

The blessings of the Lord be upon you mightily.

In Jesus' Name,

Dr. Marlene Miles

Other books by this author

AK: The Adventures of the Agape Kid

AMONG SOME THIEVES

Churchzilla, T*he Wanna-Be, Supposed-to-be Bride of Christ*

Courtroom Prayers @Midnight

Demonic Cobwebs, *Prayers Against*

Demons Hate Questions

Don't Refuse Me, Lord (4 book series)

Evil Petition in the Court of Accusation

Evil Touch

The Fold (4 book series)

    The Fold (Book 1)

    Name Your Seed (Book 2)

    The Poor Attitudes of Money (Book 3)

    Do Not Orphan Your Seed

got HEALING? Verses for Life

got LOVE? Verses for Life

got money?

How to Dental Assist

Let Me Have A Dollar's Worth

Man Safari, *The*

Marriage Ed. *Rules of Engagement & Marriage*

Made Perfect in Love

Power Money: Nine Times the Tithe

The Power of Wealth *(forthcoming)*

Prayers Against Demonic Cobwebs

Seasons of Grief

Seasons of War *(forthcoming)*

The Spirit of Poverty *(forthcoming)*

Triangular Power *(series)*

    Powers Above

    SUNBLOCK

    Do Not Swear by the Moon

    STARSTRUCK

Warfare Prayers Against Beauty Curses

Warfare Prayer Against Poverty

When the Devourer is Rebuked

The Wilderness Romance *(3-book series)*

> ***The Social Wilderness***
>
> ***The Sexual Wilderness***
>
> ***The Spiritual Wilderness***

Journals & Devotionals by this author:

The Cool of the Day – Journal for times with God

He Hears Us, Prayer Journal in 4 different colors

I Have A Star, Dream Journal kids, teen, adult

I Have A Star, Guided Prayer Journal, Boy or Girl

J'ai une Etoile, Journal des Reves

Let Her Dream, Dream Journal in multiple colors

Men Shall Dream, Dream Journal, (blue or black)

My Favorite Prayers (multiple covers)

My Sowing Journal (in three different colors)

Tengo una Estrella, Diario de Sueños

Wise Counsel (Journal in 2 styles)

Illustrated children's books by this author:

Be the Lion (3-book series)

Big Dog (8-book series)

Do Not Say That to Me

Every Apple

Fluff the Clouds

I Love You All Over the World

Imma Dance

The Jump Rope

Kiss the Sun

The Masked Man

Not During a Pandemic

Push the Wind

Slide

Tangled Taffy

What If?

Wiggle, Wiggle; Giggle, Giggle

Worry About Yourself

You Did Not Say Goodbye to Me

www.ingramcontent.com/pod-product-compliance
Lightning Source LLC
Chambersburg PA
CBHW070855050426
42453CB00012B/2209